Secrets Every Mother Should Tell Her Daughter About Life!

WORKBOOK

by Dr. Mattie Nottage

Copyright © 2015
Mattie Nottage Ministries, Int'l

Secrets Every Mother Should Tell Her Daughter About Life Workbook
by Mattie M. Nottage

Printed in the United States of America
ISBN-978-0-9896003-9-2

All rights reserved solely by author. The author guarantees all contents are original and do not infringe upon the legal rights of any other person or work. This book or parts thereof may not be reproduced in any form, stored in a retrieval system, or transmitted in any form by any means - electronic, mechanical, photocopy, recording or otherwise, without prior written permission of the author. Illustrated by Dr. Mattie Nottage

Unless otherwise indicated, all Scripture quotations are taken from the King James Study Bible ©1988 by Liberty University: Thomas Nelson Publishers, Nashville and The Amplified Bible ©1987 by the Zondervan Corporation and the Lockman Foundation, Grand Rapids, Michigan

Secrets Every Mother Should Tell Her Daughter About Life! *Workbook*

The aged women likewise,…may teach the young women…
(Titus 2:3-5)

Dedicated to ....

My dearest Magyn, Melissa, Samantha, Deandra, Dearyl, my **Girls of Excellence Program**, **Faith Village For Girls Transformation & Empowerment Initiative** and the long list of beautiful women who call me **Mother.**

- *Dr. Mattie Nottage*

#MOTHERSSECRETS

SECRETS... The Workbook

The Secrets Trilogy is now complete with the addition of the Secrets Workbook, a companion tool to the *must-read* book and journal **"Secrets Every Mother Should Tell Her Daughter About Life!"**

Who Is This Workbook For?

This workbook is an empowerment and instructional tool designed to bring positive change to the lives of young women everywhere. It can be used:

1) For personal growth and development
2) In family discussions or also during devotions
3) In group empowerment sessions, such as youth groups or girls' club meetings.
4) During civic, social or community initiatives.
5) As an instructional tool during guidance and counseling sessions.
6) In schools as a part of the curriculum for girls of all ages.

It provides excellent resource material and thought provoking questions for rich and guided discussions. Further this workbook reinforces the nugget principles and concepts shared in the companion book in order to:

1) Build strong social and moral foundations in the lives of youth.
2) Improve and enhance the overall development of good character thereby fostering better relations amongst peers.
3) Build a stronger and more vibrant community
4) Help resolve conflict amongst peers
5) Compliment Family Life, Religious Studies or Language Arts subjects in local schools.

Secrets Every Mother Should Tell Her Daughter About Life! *Workbook*

Using This Workbook

This Workbook is written in a question and answer format. Questions take the form of Short Answers, Essay Questions, Directed Writing Questions, Research and Personal Responses. By reading the corresponding nugget in the book ***Secrets*** and then completing the relevant sections in this Workbook, you will gain a deeper and better understanding of the principles presented and will be challenged to incorporate them into your daily life.

To use this workbook, read the corresponding *secret* in the book **Secrets Every Mother Should Tell Her Daughter About Life**. Secondly, using a dictionary, and Bible, research selected terms and scripture references designated in this guide and study them. This is important because the Bible admonishes us to, "**study to show yourselves approved...**" (2 Timothy 2:15). Thirdly, answer the questions in the spaces provided in the workbook.

As aforementioned, this Workbook can be used for individual or group study. When using it in a group, please share and discuss your answers and learn how to make the principles applicable to your everyday life. Moreover, work consistently and steadily through this workbook at a comfortable pace. The results will be amazing. You will note personal growth if you pray and read the Word in conjunction with applying the principles in this workbook.

So let us begin this journey of growth, development and change. From my heart to yours I share with you *"Secrets Every Mother Should Tell Her Daughter About Life! Workbook".*

With Love,
Dr. Mattie Nottage

Secrets Every Mother Should Tell Her Daughter About Life! *Workbook*

This Book Belongs To...

Name of Student: _____

Name of School: _____

Age: _____   **Grade Level:** _____

Homeroom Teacher: _____

Organization/Club: _____

Date: _____

Secrets Every Mother Should Tell Her Daughter About Life! *Workbook*

Instructions: Read *Secret* **#1 #STAYTRUE** discuss and then complete the following questions.

> *A*lways remember, and never forget...you are so special! I love and celebrate you for the gem that you are. Stay focused, stay true to God and stay true to yourself!

1. What does the statement, "You are special" mean to you?
   _____
   _____
   _____

2. Was there ever a time that you had to compromise to fit in with the crowd? If so, what was the outcome? What would you do differently now?
   _____
   _____
   _____

b. Do you see yourself as special? Yes or No. Explain
   _____
   _____
   _____
   _____
   _____

Secrets Every Mother Should Tell Her Daughter About Life! *Workbook*

3. In your opinion, what does it mean to:

a. Stay true to God:
   _____
   _____

b. Stay true to yourself:
   _____
   _____

"I will praise thee; for I am fearfully and wonderfully made..." – **Psalm 139:14**

You are a precious gem!

Secrets Every Mother Should Tell Her Daughter About Life! *Workbook*

Instructions: Read *Secret* #2 **#YOURPATHWAYOFSUCCESS** discuss and then complete the following questions.

> **D**o not allow anyone or anything to get in your pathway of success! Set your goals in life. Lock into your target and go after it!

1. In your opinion, what is a goal?
   _____
   _____

2. State at least three (3) personal goals that you wish to achieve in the following areas and then develop an action plan (*how will you accomplish these goals*) with timelines (*dates/deadlines*).

   a. Spiritual_____

   _____

   b. Academic_____

   _____

c. Personal/Social_____

_____

ACTION PLAN

_____
_____
_____
_____
_____
_____
_____
_____
_____
_____
_____
_____

3. **Project:** Make a *Goals Poster* which includes a photo of yourself and the goals listed in Question #2. Use creativity to make your poster unique and outstanding.

"I press towards the mark for the prize of the high calling of God in Christ Jesus."
- Philippians 3:14 (AMP)

Secrets Every Mother Should Tell Her Daughter About Life! *Workbook*

Instructions: Read *Secret* #3 #KEEPYOURHEART discuss and then complete the following questions.

> *M*ost men want the same thing from every woman. Never give your heart to a man except you're sure you want to spend the rest of your life with him. If you're not sure then hold on to your heart!

1. What do you think it means to give your heart to a man?
   _____
   _____
   _____
   _____

2. Why is it important, as a young lady, to hold onto your heart?
   _____
   _____
   _____

3. Give two (2) reasons why you believe some young women give their heart away to men?
   _____
   _____
   _____

Secrets Every Mother Should Tell Her Daughter About Life! *Workbook*

4a. As a young woman, why should you wait until you are more matured before dating?

_____
_____
_____

4b. At what age do you think a young lady should begin dating? Explain why.

_____
_____
_____
_____
_____
_____

"Keep thy heart with all diligence; for out of it are the issues of life." – **Proverbs 4:23**

Dating

Secrets Every Mother Should Tell Her Daughter About Life! *Workbook*

Instructions: Read *Secret* #4 **RELATIONSHIPS** discuss and then complete the following questions.

> *A*ssess all of your relationships, friendships, and associations. Enhance those that are valuable and release those that are seemingly not going anywhere. Remember, relationships do matter ... it's the good ones you should fight to maintain.

1. What qualities should you look for in a good friend? Why?

_____
_____
_____
_____
_____
_____
_____

2. What type of people/friends/associates should you stay away from? Why?

_____
_____
_____
_____
_____

Secrets Every Mother Should Tell Her Daughter About Life! *Workbook*

1. Read each conversation below. Suggest a response that would display the qualities of a ***good*** friend. Write your suggestions on the lines provided.

   Santina: Latoya, your friend Abby is really strange. I can't understand why you are friends with her. You need to kick her to the curb.

   Latoya: I guess you are right. She is really weird isn't she?

   a. As Abby's friend, a better way for Latoya to respond would be:
   _____
   _____
   _____
   _____
   _____
   _____
   _____
   _____
   _____
   _____
   _____
   _____
   _____
   _____
   _____
   _____

Secrets Every Mother Should Tell Her Daughter About Life! *Workbook*

<u>*Patrick*</u>: Ashton, let's borrow a pair of those new Nike socks from the bin. No one is watching. It's like taking candy from a baby.

<u>*Ashton*</u>: I don't want to but go ahead if you want to.

b. As Patrick's friend, a better way for Ashton to respond would have been:

_____
_____
_____
_____
_____
_____
_____

c. Gena was angry with Martha because she mistakenly stepped on her shoes. Gena wanted to fight Martha after school because she was much taller than her. What should Gena's friend, Jessica say to her about fighting Martha?

_____
_____
_____
_____
_____
_____
_____

"… get to know those who labor among you [recognize them for what they are, acknowledge and appreciate and respect them all] …" – **1 Thessalonians 5:12 (AMP)**

Secrets Every Mother Should Tell Her Daughter About Life! *Workbook*

Instructions: Read *Secret* **#5 #BEAUTYINSIDE** then discuss and complete the following questions.

> *D*o not depend on a man to tell you who you are or what you are good for in life. See beauty inside of yourself and accept whatever compliment stumbles to you along the way.

1. Why is it important to feel good about yourself and see your own inner beauty?

_____
_____
_____
_____

2. ***Take out a mirror***. Hold it up to your face and describe what you see. Do not be afraid. Tell the truth. Answer the following questions:

_____
_____
_____
_____
_____
_____
_____

Secrets Every Mother Should Tell Her Daughter About Life! *Workbook*

a) Who are you really?

_____
_____
_____
_____
_____
_____
_____

b) What are you good for in life?

_____
_____
_____
_____
_____
_____
_____

"Thou art all fair, my love; there is no spot in thee."
– **Song of Solomon 4:7 (KJV)**

Secrets Every Mother Should Tell Her Daughter About Life! *Workbook*

Unlocking The SECRETS Code
Puzzles, Games, Activities

Secrets Every Mother Should Tell Her Daughter About Life! *Workbook*

The SECRETS Revealer ACTIVITY

Directions: Unscramble each of the words below. Place the letter of the corresponding number below and uncover a clue to one of life's greatest secrets.

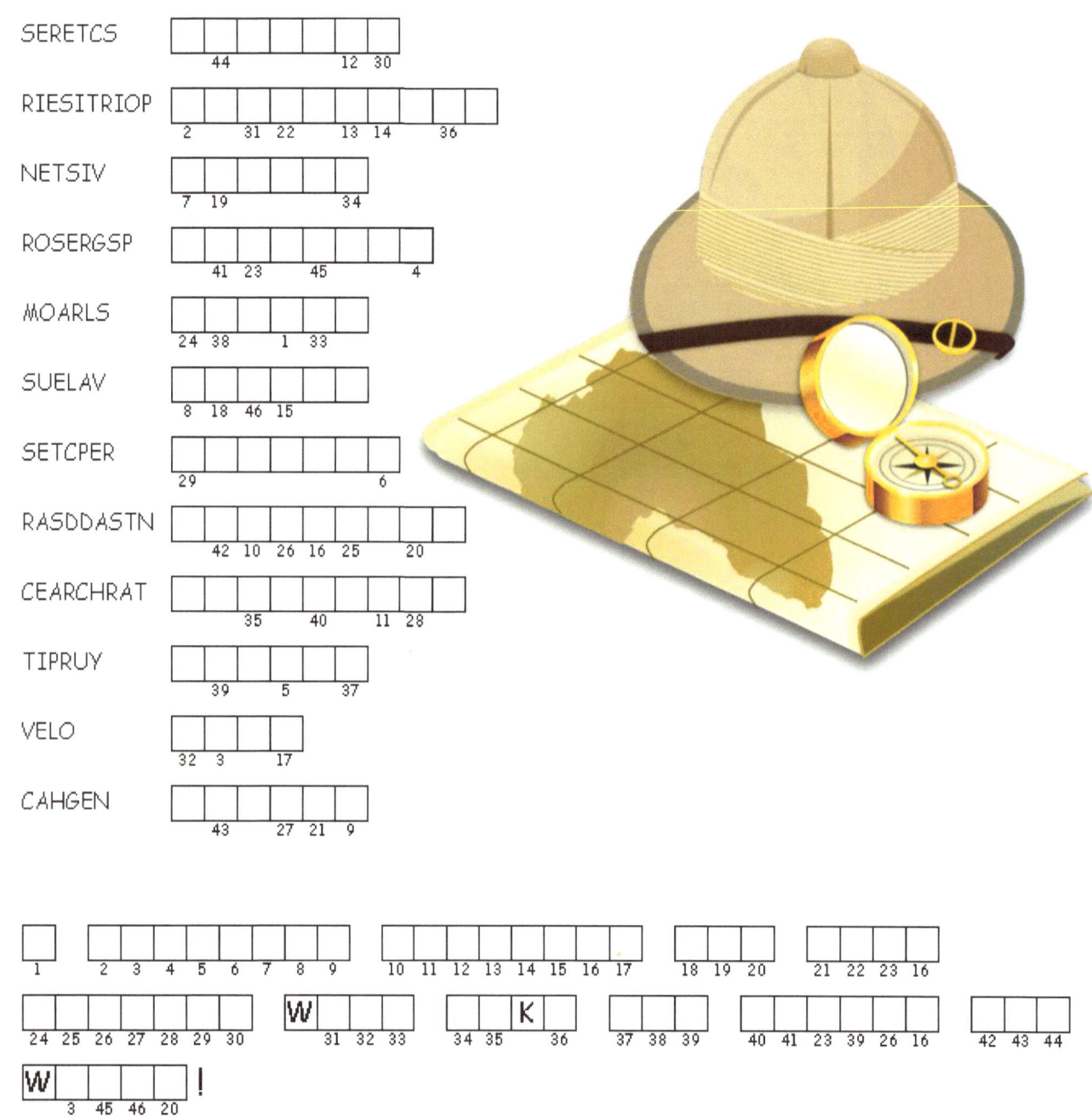

SERETCS   ☐☐☐☐☐☐☐
             44   12 30

RIESITRIOP ☐☐☐☐☐☐☐☐☐
           2   31 22 13 14   36

NETSIV   ☐☐☐☐☐☐
          7 19   34

ROSERGSP ☐☐☐☐☐☐☐☐
          41 23   45   4

MOARLS   ☐☐☐☐☐☐
          24 38 1 33

SUELAV   ☐☐☐☐☐☐
          8 18 46 15

SETCPER   ☐☐☐☐☐☐☐
          29   6

RASDDASTN ☐☐☐☐☐☐☐☐☐
          42 10 26 16 25 20

CEARCHRAT ☐☐☐☐☐☐☐☐☐
          35   40 11 28

TIPRUY   ☐☐☐☐☐☐
          39 5   37

VELO   ☐☐☐☐
          32 3 17

CAHGEN   ☐☐☐☐☐☐
          43 27 21 9

☐ ☐☐☐☐☐☐☐☐ ☐☐☐☐☐☐☐☐ ☐☐☐ ☐☐☐
1 2 3 4 5 6 7 8 9 10 11 12 13 14 15 16 17 18 19 20 21 22 23 16

☐☐☐☐☐☐☐ W☐☐ ☐K☐ ☐☐☐ ☐☐☐☐☐☐ ☐☐☐
24 25 26 27 28 29 30 31 32 33 34 35 36 37 38 39 40 41 23 39 26 16 42 43 44

W☐☐☐!
3 45 46 20

20

Secrets Every Mother Should Tell Her Daughter About Life! *Workbook*

Instructions: Read *Secret* **#7 #PRICELESS** then discuss and complete the following question(s).

> *I*f you see yourself as priceless, you will never be ***bought or sold*** by anyone. In other words, you must value yourself and others will value you.

To value yourself means to have high regard, respect for or esteem for oneself based on Secret #7.

1. According to Secret #7, to value yourself means to have respect for or esteem for oneself. In your opinion, do you value yourself? ☐ Yes or ☐ No

2. What does it mean to value yourself?
   _____
   _____

3. State five (5) reasons why you DO or DO NOT value yourself. Tick and complete which is more true to you.

☐ **Yes, I do value myself**   ☐ **No, I do not value myself**

1. _____   1. _____
2. _____   2. _____
3. _____   3. _____
4. _____   4. _____
5. _____   5. _____

"But [you] are a chosen generation, a royal priesthood, an holy nation, a peculiar people..." - **1 Peter 2:9**

Secrets Every Mother Should Tell Her Daughter About Life! *Workbook*

Instructions: Read *Secret* #9 **#SEIZEOPPORTUNITIES** discuss and then complete the following questions.

> *S*eize every door of opportunity ... go through it with boldness. DO NOT PROCRASTINATE! Doors open but they can also close.

1. What does it mean to procrastinate?
_____
_____
_____

2. What are some of the opportunities that have come your way that you did not take advantage of? Why?
_____
_____
_____

3. *Fear seems to be one of the factors that prevents people from walking through doors of opportunity.* Do you agree or disagree? Discuss.
_____
_____
_____
_____

"Making the very most of the time [buying up each opportunity], because the days are evil."
– Ephesians 5:16 (AMP)

Secrets Every Mother Should Tell Her Daughter About Life! *Workbook*

Instructions: Read *Secret* **#10 #PROCRASTINATION** discuss and then complete the following questions.

> *P*rocrastination is expensive, and will cost too much to pay for *later*. Do everything in the time allotted. Do not waste a minute, make good on every opportunity.

1. What is an opportunity?

_____
_____

2. Share a time when you procrastinated concerning doing something important. What was the outcome? What lesson did you learn?

_____
_____
_____
_____
_____
_____
_____

"Yet a little sleep, a little slumber, a little folding of the hands to sleep: So shall thy poverty come...as an armed man." – **Proverbs 6:10, 11 (KJV)**

Secrets Every Mother Should Tell Her Daughter About Life! *Workbook*

Instructions: Read *Secret* #13 #SAVEYOURSELF4MARRIAGE discuss and then complete the following questions.

> ℬeing a virgin is a good thing. Never allow anyone to belittle or humiliate you because you choose to save yourself for marriage. After all, your virginity is the **token of purity** God gave you – guard it with your life.

1. What does it mean to be a virgin?
   _____
   _____
   _____

2. Are you still a virgin? Yes or No
   _____
   _____

3. In your opinion, what is the importance of remaining a virgin until marriage?
   _____
   _____
   _____
   _____
   _____

Secrets Every Mother Should Tell Her Daughter About Life! *Workbook*

4. What advice would you give to a friend who has lost her virginity?

   _____
   _____
   _____
   _____
   _____

5. Complete the following chart.

What do you think are the advantages of keeping your virginity until marriage	*What do you think are the disadvantages of losing your virginity prior to marriage? (Engaging in pre-marital sex)*

"For this is the will of God, even your sanctification, that ye should abstain from fornication."
– **1 Thessalonians 4:3**

Secrets Every Mother Should Tell Her Daughter About Life! *Workbook*

Instructions: Read *Secret* **#16 #STANDARDS** then discuss and then complete the following questions.

> *H*aving sex with someone who is not your husband simply means, you have lowered your standards, and have ***sold yourself short!***

1. In your own words, what does it mean to have standards?
_____
_____

2. What are some of the standards that you have set for yourself as a young lady?
_____
_____
_____

3. Why do you think that it is important to have high moral standards as a single person and even in marriage?
_____
_____
_____
_____
_____
_____

"Nevertheless, to avoid fornication, let every man have his own wife, and let every woman have her own husband." – **1 Corinthians 7:2**

Secrets Every Mother Should Tell Her Daughter About Life! *Workbook*

Instructions: Read *Secret* **#17 #DONOTBEMISLED** discuss and then complete the following questions.

> *D*o not let people lead you where you do not want to go!

1. *You are known by the company that you keep.* Agree or Disagree? Discuss.
_____
_____
_____

2. The lives of many young women have been led away and destroyed because of peer pressure. Define the word(s) *peer* and *peer pressure*. Then give an example of each type of pressure (positive and negative).
_____
_____
_____
_____

3. Identify five ways to resist negative peer pressure.

a._____
b._____
c._____
d._____
e._____

Do not be deceived: "Bad company corrupts good morals." - **1 Corinthians 15:33 (AMP)**

Secrets Every Mother Should Tell Her Daughter About Life! *Workbook*

Instructions: Read *Secret* **#22 #RELEASEPEOPLE** discuss and then complete the following questions.

> **R**elease those people who have no intentions of changing. If they are not an asset today they will certainly be a liability tomorrow.

1. In your own words, state what **Secret #22** means to you, emphasizing and further defining the words *asset* **(someone that is helpful)** and *liability* **(someone that is not helpful)** in context.

_____
_____
_____
_____
_____
_____
_____
_____
_____
_____
_____
_____
_____
_____

"Be ye not unequally yoked with unbelievers: for what fellowship hath righteousness with unrighteousness, light with darkness?" – **2 Corinthians 6:14**

Secrets Every Mother Should Tell Her Daughter About Life! *Workbook*

Instructions: Read *Secret* **#23 #WALKAWAYFROMABUSE** discuss and then complete the following questions.

> *D*o not allow anyone to abuse you! Physical, mental, verbal, emotional, or sexual abuse is unacceptable, and should not be tolerated. Pray, forgive and, if necessary, find the courage to walk away. Never feel obligated to stay long enough to become a victim.

1. Abuse is said to be the abnormal or wrong use of something that causes it to become damaged, ineffective or unproductive. Explain with examples, the following types of abuse:

TYPE OF ABUSE	DESCRIPTION
Physical:	
Emotional/Mental:	
Verbal:	
Sexual:	

Secrets Every Mother Should Tell Her Daughter About Life! *Workbook*

1. Have you or anyone you know ever suffered any type of abuse? Yes or No? Explain.
   _____
   _____
   _____

2. Suggest at least three (3) persons or agencies that can provide help for abused victims and state the type of assistance they provide.
   For example: The Women's Crisis Center for Counseling

Agency/Person	Assistance
1.	
2.	
3.	

3. What advice would you give to a friend who is being abused?
   _____
   _____
   _____
   _____
   _____
   _____

"As for a person who stirs up division, after warning him once and then twice, have nothing more to do with him."
- Titus 3:10 (ESV)

Secrets Every Mother Should Tell Her Daughter About Life! *Workbook*

Instructions: Read *Secret* **#24 #CHANGE4PROGRESS** discuss and then complete the following questions.

> *C*hange is necessary for your progress. If you're going to move forward, you must be willing to embrace change.

1. What does the word *change* mean?

_____
_____
_____
_____
_____

2. What does the statement *change is necessary for your progress* mean to you?

_____
_____
_____
_____
_____
_____
_____

3. How have you grown or experienced positive change as a young person over the last year?

_____
_____
_____

4. State and discus two (2) examples of positive change that can benefit your family, church and country.

Recipients of Change	Positive Change
Family 	1. 2.
Church 	1. 2.
School 	1. 2.
Country	1. 2.

"...be ye transformed by the renewing of your mind..." - **Romans 12:2**

Secrets Every Mother Should Tell Her Daughter About Life! *Workbook*

Instructions: Read *Secret* **#25 #PERSONALINDEPENDENCE** then discuss and complete the following questions.

> *L*earn how to cook, clean, iron and change your own car's tire. Personal independence is powerful, and should never be mistaken as female dominance. Gracefully celebrate being a woman and decide to be the ***best*** woman you can be.

1. Relative to Secret #25, what are some of the life skills that you have learnt? Why are they important?

_____
_____
_____

2. In the future, should you get married and have a daughter, what are some of the life skills and life lessons that you would impart to her?

_____
_____
_____
_____
_____
_____
_____

Today is gonna BEE a SWEET DAY!

"A good woman is hard to find, and worth far more than diamonds." – **Proverbs 31:10 (MSG)**

Secrets Every Mother Should Tell Her Daughter About Life! *Workbook*

Instructions: Read *Secret* #27 #3WPURPOSEFACTORS then discuss and then complete the following questions.

> *L*earn the 3-W's which govern the **PURPOSE FACTORS of life!**
>
> Know... *W*ho you are.
>
> *W*hy are you here?
>
> *W*here are you going?

1. Who you have become is the sum total of your God-given characteristics coupled with whatever you have experienced in life. Therefore with this in mind, who are you?

_____
_____
_____

2. Why are you here? What do you believe that you are on earth for?

_____
_____
_____
_____

3. Where are you going in life?

_____
_____
_____
_____

"By having the eyes of your understanding enlightened, you can know and understand the hope to which He has called you..." - **Ephesians 1:18**

Secrets Every Mother Should Tell Her Daughter About Life! *Workbook*

Instructions: Read *Secret* **#29 #GETBACKINTHEFIGHT** then discuss and complete the following questions.

> *I*f for some strange reason you make a mistake, or fall…
> GET UP! **NEVER STAY DOWN!**
> The seal of champions is in their ability to bounce back after they have been knocked down. You are a champion. Don't Quit and Get Back In The Fight!

1. *Failure is not final….agree or disagree?*

_____
_____
_____
_____

b. Name three (3) people that you know of in the world who are examples of getting up after being knocked down.

    i. _____

    ii. _____

    iii. _____

2. How would you respond in the following situations?

a. You got a failing grade on your midterm exam:

_____
_____
_____

Secrets Every Mother Should Tell Her Daughter About Life! *Workbook*

b. You dropped the baton and came in last in a race you should have won:
_____
_____
_____

c. You tried out for the basketball team but was not selected:
_____
_____
_____

d. You tried to befriend someone you really liked in school but they rejected your friendship:
_____
_____
_____

"And let us not grow weary of doing good, for in due season we will reap, if we do not give up."
 – Galatians 6:9 (ESV)

Instructions: Read *Secret* **#34 #TAKINGADVICE** discuss and then complete the following questions.

> **O**nly take advice from people that have walked that road before. Listening to inexperienced novices will lead you in pot holes, pitfalls and unbelievable dead-ends.

1. In your opinion what is a pothole, pitfall or dead end in life?

_____
_____
_____
_____
_____
_____

2. How can you avoid them?

_____
_____
_____
_____
_____
_____
_____

Secrets Every Mother Should Tell Her Daughter About Life! *Workbook*

3. The book of Proverbs is full of wisdom. **Proverbs 13:1** says that a wise son will heed his father's instructions. Look up and write out nine (9) other verses from the Bible that speaks about receiving wise counsel. The book of Proverbs is a good place to start.

1. **Proverbs 13:1**: A wise son heareth his father's instruction: but a scorner heareth not rebuke.

2. _____
3. _____
4. _____
5. _____
6. _____
7. _____
8. _____
9. _____
10. _____

"The way of fools seems right to them, but the wise listen to godly advice." – **Proverbs 12:1 (ASV)**

Secrets Every Mother Should Tell Her Daughter About Life! *Workbook*

Instructions: Read *Secret* **#35 #YOURNUMBER1FAN** discuss and then complete the following questions.

> *I*f no-one applauds you for what you felt was a stellar performance, find a mirror and applaud yourself. Be your #1 fan.

1. In your opinion, how important is accepting yourself and having high self-esteem?

_____
_____
_____
_____
_____
_____
_____
_____

2. Everyone needs encouragement sometimes. However, are you self-motivated? Or do you need constant affirmation from others?

_____
_____
_____
_____
_____
_____
_____
_____

"... but David encouraged himself in the Lord his God..." – **1 Samuel 30:6**

Secrets Every Mother Should Tell Her Daughter About Life! *Workbook*

Instructions: Read *Secret* **#39 #WORTHANDVALUE** discuss and then complete the following questions.

> *A*nything that's worth doing in life, if you add value to it, you can do it!
>
> *V*alue = time, effort, investment, energy, commitment, money, worth, faith, dedication, priority.

Your goals in life are valuable. Imagine that you are planning a *Values For Life!* campaign for your youth group or school. Write three (3) possible slogans about values for life on the numbered lines. Choose the slogan that you prefer most and place it on the banner below. Then decorate your banner to illustrate your slogan. Also, state why you choose that particular slogan.

Slogan 1: _____

Slogan 2: _____

Slogan 3: _____

  I chose this slogan because:_____

_____

"[Be] not slothful in business; fervent in spirit;..." – **Romans 12:11**

Secrets Every Mother Should Tell Her Daughter About Life! *Workbook*

Instructions: Read *Secret* **#41 #YOUAREANEAGLE** discuss and then complete the following questions.

> *E*agles fly high! Others waste time pecking and chirping over bird droppings. Decide whether you are in the company of eagles, or in the circle of others! I'd rather be a high-flying eagle than a low-pecking chicken.

1. *Birds of a feather flock together*. What kind of people do you hang out with? Explain.
___
___
___
___
___

2. What are your friends saying about you as an individual?
___
___
___

3. Evaluate your friends. What steps would you take to **de-chicken** your life?
___
___
___
___

"But they that wait upon the Lord shall renew their strength; they shall mount up with wings as eagles;..." - **Isaiah 40:31**

41

Secrets Every Mother Should Tell Her Daughter About Life! *Workbook*

Instructions: Read *Secret* #42 #PERSONALPRUDENCE discuss and th complete the following questions.

> *E*xercise discretion in your everyday life. Be cautious of people with whom you surround yourself, especially those called "friends." Personal prudence should take precedence in everything that you do.

1. **YOU ARE IN THE CENTER OF THE CIRCLE.** Evaluate your friendships completing the following chart. Identify the top two persons who are in your in circle? Who needs to be removed? Who needs to be added?

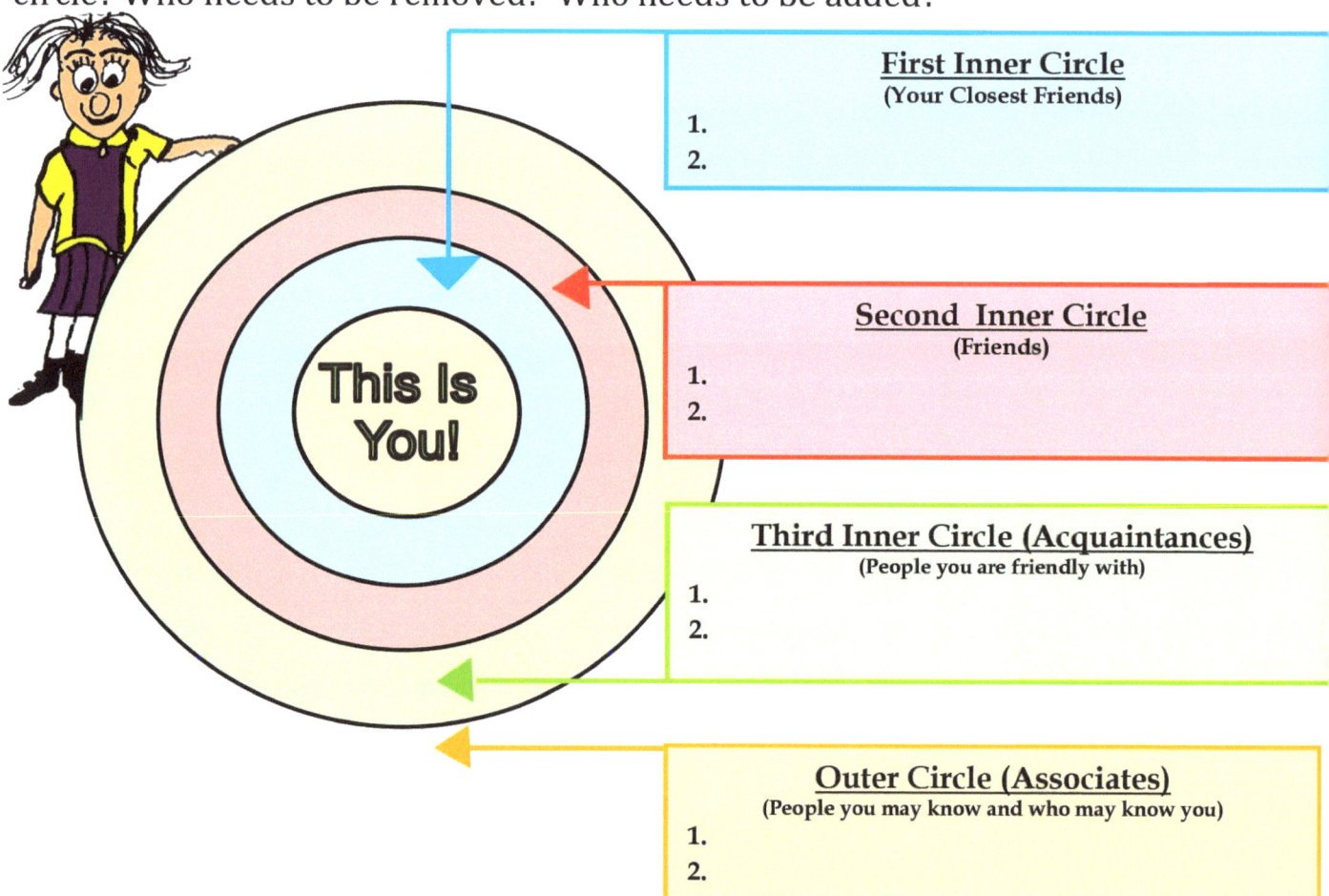

First Inner Circle
(Your Closest Friends)
1.
2.

Second Inner Circle
(Friends)
1.
2.

Third Inner Circle (Acquaintances)
(People you are friendly with)
1.
2.

Outer Circle (Associates)
(People you may know and who may know you)
1.
2.

"I, Wisdom...make prudence my dwelling..." – **Proverbs 8:12 (AMP)**

Secrets Every Mother Should Tell Her Daughter About Life! *Workbook*

Instructions: Read *Secret* **#44 #PERSEVERANCE** discuss and then complete the following questions.

> *G*iving up is never an option! Perseverance is the order of the day that will eventually lead you to your destiny.

1. **This exercise can be done as an individual or a group**. Write and perform a rap, song or poem based on the theme of *perseverance*. Your song or poem can be free verse or rhyming in style. Use creativity for extra points.

___

___

___

___

___

___

___

___

___

___

___

___

___

___

___

"For the vision is yet for an appointed time,...: though it tarry, wait for it; because it will surely come, it will not tarry." – **Habakkuk 2:3**

Instructions: Read *Secret* **#45 #GETYOURGOLD** discuss and then complete the following questions.

> *E*veryone is not ordained to go with you to the top. Leave some people at the foot of the mountain. Go up and get your gold.
> They will be right there on your way back down.

1. *Go up and get your gold!* What are some of the short term and long term goals, dreams or aspirations that you are working towards academically, spiritually and socially?

Academically:
_____
_____
_____

Spiritually:
_____
_____
_____

Socially:
_____
_____
_____

"Set your affection on things above, not on things on the earth." – **Colossians 3:2**

Secrets Every Mother Should Tell Her Daughter About Life! *Workbook*

Instructions: Read *Secret* **#46 #FOCUSONYOURFUTURE** discuss and then complete the following questions.

> *Y*ou cannot change your past, but you can do everything about your now, and your future. Your greatest seasons are before you. Move forward!

What are some of the things that hindered you in the past?	Analyze your present situation or disposition.	Where do you see yourself headed in the future?
1.		
2.		
3.		
4.		

"...forgetting those things which are behind, and reaching forth unto those things which are before..." – **Philippians 3:13**

Secrets Every Mother Should Tell Her Daughter About Life! *Workbook*

Instructions: Read *Secret* **#48 #YOURDESTINY** discuss and then complete the following questions.

> **D**estiny is where you are headed. Until then, celebrate where you are now!

1. **Group Work.** (Activity can be divided into several groups.) Additional points will be given for stage props/crafts and costumes.

Activity: I believe that any road can take you anywhere, but the right road will take you exactly where you need to be. Where do you see yourself twenty (20) years from now? Produce and perform a brief five (5) minute skit/drama depicting what life would be like then. *(Use extra folder sheets if necessary.)*

_____
_____
_____
_____

For the vision [is] yet for an appointed time, but at the end it shall speak, and not lie..." - **Habbakuk 2:3**

Secrets Every Mother Should Tell Her Daughter About Life! *Workbook*

Instructions: Read *Secret* **#50 #GLEANFROMOTHERS** discuss and then complete the following questions.

> *T*ake time to learn new things. Glean from people who have experience. If you feel you already know everything, then you are a sad commentary we will all soon read about.

1. Many persons such as a teacher, pastor or parent may have positively impacted your life. Write a letter of appreciating thanking them for the role they have played in changing your life.

_____
_____
_____
_____
_____
_____
_____
_____
_____
_____
_____
_____
_____
_____
_____

"A wise [person] will hear, and will increase learning; and a person of understanding shall attain unto wise counsels:" - **Proverbs 1:5**

Instructions: Read *Secret* #55 #LEARNFROMOTHERS discuss and then complete the following questions.

> *E*xperience is not always the greatest teacher. Learn from other people's mistakes and successes.

1. Identify some of the mistakes and successes that you can learn from people around you that will assist you in getting to your destiny?

Failures of Family/Friends
- _____
- _____
- _____
- _____
- _____

Successes of Family/Friends
- _____
- _____
- _____
- _____
- _____

"These things happened to them as examples and were written down as warnings for us,..."
– 1 Corinthians 10:11 (NIV)

Secrets Every Mother Should Tell Her Daughter About Life! *Workbook*

Instructions: Read *Secret* **#46 #DREAMSVISIONSIDEAS** discuss and then complete the following questions.

> **D**reams, visions and ideas are all a part of God's plan to get you safely to your destiny.
> Dream your dreams; see visions and put motion to your ideas.

1. If you were Einstein or Harriet Tubman and you found yourself stuck at a crossroads in life, write a prayer asking God to give you a dream, a vision and an idea to take you to your destiny or road to success.

"For I know the plans *and* thoughts that I have for you, says the Lord" – **Jeremiah 29:11 (AMP)**

Secrets Every Mother Should Tell Her Daughter About Life! *Workbook*

Instructions: Read *Secret* **#63 #THEBETTERYOU** discuss and then complete the following questions.

> *C*haracter is really who you are.
> Spend quality time enhancing the ***better*** you.

1. Name and define six of the pillars of character.

Pillars of Character	Definition/Illustration
1.	
2.	
3.	
4.	
5.	
6.	

2. Which character trait(s) do you need to develop more in your life? Why?

_____
_____
_____
_____

"The LORD will perfect that which concerneth me..." – **Psalm 138:8**

Secrets Every Mother Should Tell Her Daughter About Life! *Workbook*

Instructions: Read *Secret* **#64 #LEAVEAGOODMEMORY** discuss and then complete the following questions.

> **P**eople will always remember who you are, more than what you do! First impressions are lasting so leave a good memory in the minds of those you meet.

Describe an experience that you have had meeting someone new or going into a new experience (e.g. first day at a new school, on a job training experience, etc.) that left a lasting impression. Was it a negative or positive one? Why?

_____
_____
_____
_____
_____
_____
_____
_____
_____
_____
_____
_____
_____
_____
_____

"The memory of the just is blessed:..." – **Proverbs 10:7**

Instructions: Read *Secret* #65 #HARDWORK discuss and then complete the following questions.

> *A* little bit of hard work will not kill you. Work hard early. You'll have time to rest, relax, and enjoy life later.

Devise a daily schedule, allotting time for doing homework, studying for tests or exams, house work, personal devotion time, etc.

TIME	SUNDAY	MONDAY	TUESDAY	WEDNESDAY	THURSDAY	FRIDAY	SATURDAY
6:00 a.m.							
7:00 a.m.							
8:00 a.m.							
9:00 a.m.							
10:00 a.m.							
11:00 a.m.							
12:00 (noon)							
1:00 p.m.							
2:00 p.m.							
3:00 p.m.							
4:00 p.m.							
5:00 p.m.							
6:00 p.m.							
7:00 p.m.							
8:00 p.m.							
9:00 p.m.							

"I must work the works of him that sent me, while it is day: the night cometh, when no man can work."

- John 9:4

Secrets Every Mother Should Tell Her Daughter About Life! *Workbook*

Unlocking The SECRETS Code
Puzzles, Games, Activities

Secrets Every Mother Should Tell Her Daughter About Life! *Workbook*

The SECRETS Message Find

Directions: Special secret words are hidden in the group of letters below. See how quickly you can find them?

Y	S	Y	A	R	E	S	P	E	C	T	O	U	A	P
N	T	E	R	C	E	G	A	O	D	S	G	R	R	E
I	F	I	I	A	H	T	T	E	S	T	M	O	I	Y
T	A	R	L	T	T	I	R	A	C	L	C	E	T	A
S	V	S	I	I	I	Z	E	C	G	R	R	I	E	E
E	O	S	T	E	B	N	H	V	A	R	R	R	S	S
D	R	U	U	R	N	A	U	S	E	U	R	O	U	S
B	D	C	G	E	R	D	T	T	P	M	P	T	B	T
E	F	O	Z	D	V	I	S	N	R	R	E	Y	A	A
B	U	F	S	A	N	T	D	H	U	O	H	N	W	N
L	Q	H	L	A	D	M	P	P	I	O	P	N	T	D
U	I	U	T	S	L	A	I	R	T	P	C	P	Y	A
P	E	I	P	R	O	G	R	E	S	S	S	C	O	R
S	O	P	R	A	C	T	I	C	E	C	P	B	A	D
N	E	C	N	A	R	E	V	E	S	R	E	P	B	S

ABUSE	ACCOUNTABILITY	ACHIEVEMENT
ATTITUDE	DESTINY	FAVOR
FOCUS	FRIENDSHIPS	HARDSHIP
OPPORTUNITIES	PERSEVERANCE	PRACTICE
PROCRASTINATION	PROGRESS	PURITY
PURPOSE	RESPECT	STANDARDS
TRIALS	VALUES	

54

Secrets Every Mother Should Tell Her Daughter About Life! *Workbook*

Instructions: Read *Secret* **#67 #MORALSANDPRINCIPLES** discuss and then complete the following questions.

> *M*orals and principles help to govern your decisions. Life without morals is like an out-of-control train destined for a wreck, which eventually ends up nowhere.

1. What are morals?

_____
_____
_____

2. Does your family have morals and principles for life that they live by?
☐ Yes   ☐ No

Discuss some of the morals and principles which govern your life.

_____
_____
_____
_____
_____
_____
_____
_____

"But when He, the Spirit of Truth (the Truth-giving Spirit) comes, He will guide you into all the Truth (the whole, full Truth)" – **John 16:13 (AMP)**

Secrets Every Mother Should Tell Her Daughter About Life! *Workbook*

Instructions: Read *Secret* **#78 #SAVEANDINVEST** discuss and then complete the following questions.

> *L*earn how to save, but know when to invest. Good investments will always yield a good return.

1. **Stick to your budget.** You are never too young to begin saving and to develop a budget. Create a budget control sheet for yourself. List your income (eg. allowance, lunch money, part time job, etc.) and your expenses (eg. Bus fare, lunch money, clothes/uniform shopping).

BUDGETING YOUR MONEY		
INCOME:		
DESCRIPTION	AMOUNT	**Calculations**
Allowance/Lunch Money		
Birthday Money		
Other:		
TOTAL INCOME	$	
EXPENDITURE:		
DESCRIPTION	AMOUNT	
Tithes/Offering/Love Gifts	$	
EXPENSES:		
DESCRIPTION	AMOUNT	
DAILY NEEDS:		
Cell Phone(phone cards, data, etc.)		
Groceries/Snacks		
BUS FEE:		
SHOPPING:		
Clothes		
Other Shopping		
FUN:		
Entertainment (Movies, pizza, etc.)		
Other Expenses:		
TOTAL EXPENSES/EXPENDITURE	$	
PROFIT/LOSS (Total INCOME Minus EXPENSES) = $		

"Cast your bread upon the waters for you will find it after many days." – **Ecclesiastes 11:1**

Secrets Every Mother Should Tell Her Daughter About Life! *Workbook*

Instructions: Read *Secret* **#79** **#ALWAYSRESPECTTIME** discuss and then complete the following questions.

> *N*ever disrespect time. If you do, time will disrespect and embarrass you ... *at the wrong time!*

1. Are you a person who respects time? Are you constantly on time?

_____
_____
_____
_____

2. What would be the consequences of constantly being late?

_____
_____
_____

3. How can you improve your time management?

_____
_____
_____

"To every season there is a purpose and a time for everything under the heavens"
– **Ecclesiastes. 3:1**

Secrets Every Mother Should Tell Her Daughter About Life! *Workbook*

Instructions: Read *Secret* **#91 #RESPECTISEARNED** discuss and then complete the following questions.

> **R**espect cannot be bought or sold ... it must be earned!

1. Define the term *respect.*
   _____
   _____

2. *In order to get respect, you must give respect.* Agree or disagree. Why?
   _____
   _____
   _____
   _____
   _____
   _____
   _____
   _____

3. *Some young people today lack respect, especially for elders.* Agree or disagree. Explain.
   _____
   _____
   _____

"Therefore all things whatsoever ye would that men should do to you, do you even so to them:"
– Matthew 7:12

Secrets Every Mother Should Tell Her Daughter About Life! *Workbook*

Instructions: Read *Secret* #95 **#DISCIPLINEISPRIORITY** discuss and then complete the following questions.

> *D*iscipline should be your #1 priority of the day. Train yourself to do that which is right. Stick to your plans unless changing them brings you closer to your goals.

1. In your own words, define the term discipline.
_____
_____

2. How can being a disciplined person benefit your life or be an advantage?

_____
_____
_____
_____
_____
_____

3. List three (3) professions that you feel require strong levels of discipline. (For example, Police Officers…)

    a. _____

    b. _____

    c. _____

"He that [hath] no rule over his own spirit [is like] a city [that is] broken down, [and] without walls."
- Proverbs 25:28

Secrets Every Mother Should Tell Her Daughter About Life! *Workbook*

Instructions: Read **Secret #101** **#DELAYISNOTDENIAL** discuss and then complete the following questions.

> **D**elay doesn't mean denial. Patiently wait a while. Everything God has promised you will come to pass exactly as He said.

1. What does it mean to *patiently* wait for something?
_____
_____

2. List at least three (3) of the promises of God from His Word that concerns you. For example, God promises to bless them that bless you.

PROMISE(S) OF GOD	SCRIPTURE REFERENCE
1.	
2.	
3.	

"For yet a little while, and He that shall come; will come and will not tarry." – **Hebrews 10:37**

Secrets Every Mother Should Tell Her Daughter About Life! *Workbook*

Instructions: Read *Secret* #102 #KEEPYOURAREACLEAN discuss and then complete the following questions.

> *A*lways keep your surroundings clean. Don't give anyone the *privilege* of cleaning up your mess!

1. Do you consider yourself to be a clean or tidy person? What can you do to keep your surroundings clean?

a. **Home:**
_____
_____

b. **Community:**
_____
_____

2. What can you do to help keep your school clean?
_____
_____
_____

3. What improvements are needed by your neighborhood or community which are at a governmental level? Write a letter to your Member of Parliament or Local Government Agency and agitate for improvements in your community such as a new park, frequent trash collection, etc. (Write your response on the next page. Use additional folder sheets as necessary.)

Secrets Every Mother Should Tell Her Daughter About Life! *Workbook*

Answer for Question #3:

"The wise woman builds her house,..." – **Proverbs 14:1 (NLT)**

Secrets Every Mother Should Tell Her Daughter About Life! *Workbook*

Instructions: Read *Secret* #103 **#MAKEOTHERSRESPONSIBLE** discuss and then complete the following questions.

> *T*ake responsibility for your own actions and make others accountable for theirs!

ACCOUNTABILITY....

1. How responsible or accountable are you? Examine the following scenarios and then provide a response.

a. Your best friend got some tickets to see your favorite band in concert tonight. However, you have a major project due in morning and you have not finished. What do you do?

_____
_____
_____
_____
_____

b. It is your group's turn to visit the Senior Citizens Home and complete some yard work for your community service hours for graduation. However, there is a new movie out that you want to see at the mall. What do you do?

_____
_____
_____
_____

"Wherefore comfort yourselves together, and edify one another..." – **1 Thessalonians 5:11**

Secrets Every Mother Should Tell Her Daughter About Life! *Workbook*

Instructions: Read *Secret* **#104 #TAKERESPONSIBILITY** from the book *Secrets,* discuss and then complete the following questions.

> *N*ever blame people for something you had the power to change yourself. Take responsibility for what happened.

1. Taking responsibility is a part of maturity. Agree or disagree? Discuss.

_____
_____
_____

2. Is there a particular subject that you constantly fail in? What do you feel is the possible reason for failure? What can you do to take responsibility for the failure? And how can you correct that now and in the future?

_____
_____
_____
_____
_____
_____
_____
_____

"For every man shall bear his own burden." – **Galatians 6:5**

Secrets Every Mother Should Tell Her Daughter About Life! *Workbook*

Instructions: Read *Secret* **#107 #NEVERBELIEVEALIE** discuss and then complete the following questions.

> *N*ever believe a lie, especially when truth is looking you right in the face.

1. What is a lie?

   _____
   _____
   _____

2. Why do you think it is sometimes easier for you to believe a lie rather than the truth?

   _____
   _____
   _____

3. Write out two scriptures about telling the truth.

   _____
   _____

4. Give an account or example of an incident where you could have lied, but you told the truth instead – what was the outcome?

   _____
   _____

"Then you will know the truth, and the truth will set you free." – **John 8:32 (ESV)**

Secrets Every Mother Should Tell Her Daughter About Life! *Workbook*

Instructions: Read *Secret* **#113 #STANDFORWHATYOUBELIEVE** from the book *Secrets,* discuss and then complete the following questions.

> *N*ever be afraid to stand alone, especially if it is for something you believe. The crowd is not always right.

1. **Rosa Parks** was an individual who had to stand for what she believed. In a separate folder, complete a research project on this individual. Who was she? What stand did she take? How did this stand affect her life and generation?

_____
_____
_____

2. Discuss a time that you had to stand for something that was morally or spiritually sound. What were the circumstances? What was the outcome?

_____
_____
_____
_____

"Be alert and on your guard. Stand firm in your faith." – **1 Corinthians 16:13 (AMP)**

Secrets Every Mother Should Tell Her Daughter About Life! *Workbook*

Instructions: Read *Secret* **#120 #PRACTICE$SUCCESS** discuss and then complete the following questions.

> *P*ractice, practice, practice!
> Hours of practice will always pay you back
> with favor and good success.

1. *Practice makes perfect.* Agree or disagree? Discuss.

_____
_____
_____
_____
_____

2. List some things that you need to practice to perfect, then start practicing.

a._____

b._____

c._____

d._____

e._____

"Study to shew thyself approved unto God, a workman that needeth not to be ashamed, rightly dividing the word of truth" - 2 Timothy 2:**15**

Secrets Every Mother Should Tell Her Daughter About Life! *Workbook*

Instructions: Read **Secret #137 #THERIGHTATTITUDE**, discuss and then complete the following questions.

> **S**mell good, look great, dress well, speak confidently and modestly! But whatever you do, keep the right attitude. A good character will be remembered long after your perfume wears off!

1. Why is it important to have the right attitude?

_____
_____
_____

2. In your opinion, what does **Pumpkin** suggest or mean by this **Attitude Nugget**? (Write your answer on the next page. Use additional folder sheets if necessary.)

Attitude Nugget
Just as paint adds color and style to a house so does your attitude add color and style to your character.

Pumpkin

68

Secrets Every Mother Should Tell Her Daughter About Life! *Workbook*

"Be completely humble and gentle; be patient, bearing with one another in love." – **Ephesians 4:2 (NIV)**

Secrets Every Mother Should Tell Her Daughter About Life! *Workbook*

Instructions: Read **Secret #149 #DONOTWASTETIME** discuss and then complete the following questions.

> **M**ost young people have misconceived notions, that they have plenty of time, and if by some strange chance they run out of it, they believe they can buy more. Not So!
> Wasted time can never be regained, not even on sale, not even at a thrift store.

1. *Time waits for no man.* Agree or disagree. Discuss

Time will not stop for Man

_____
_____
_____
_____
_____
_____
_____
_____
_____
_____

Walk in wisdom toward them that are without, redeeming the time. – **Colossians 4:5 (ESV)**

Secrets Every Mother Should Tell Her Daughter About Life! *Workbook*

Instructions: Read *Secret* **#150 #SURROUNDYOURSELFWITH THERIGHT PEOPLE** discuss and then complete the following questions.

> Surround yourself with people who at least have an idea about your dreams. People who have no idea of who you are, and where you are going tend to take you in the wrong direction.

1. Do you feel that you have good people around you? Are they helping to push you in the right direction? What are you plans for the future? Are you going straight into the workforce after graduation? Are you going to college? How will you get there? Discuss.

_____
_____
_____

2. Who are some of the people who will be instrumental in you achieving your goals or realizing your plans? What part do they play in your life?

_____
_____
_____

"Where no counsel is, the people fall: but in the multitude of counsellors there is safety."
– **Proverbs 11:14**

Secrets Every Mother Should Tell Her Daughter About Life! *Workbook*

Instructions: Read *Secret* **#162 #FINDINGYOURPURPOSE** discuss and then complete the following questions.

> *I*f you have not yet identified that thing which **consumes your mind, your prayers and even your finances; which keeps you up at night;** ...then I propose to you that *you have not found your purpose in life*!

1. In your opinion, what is purpose?

_____
_____
_____
_____

2. Study the diagram below. What do you believe is your purpose in life? Analyze and discuss. (Write your answer on the next page. Use additional folder sheets if necessary.)

Secrets Every Mother Should Tell Her Daughter About Life! *Workbook*

"For we are His workmanship created in Christ Jesus unto good works which God has before ordained that we should walk in them." - **Ephesians 2:10**

Secrets Every Mother Should Tell Her Daughter About Life! *Workbook*

Instructions: Read *Secret* **#159 #EMBRACINGLIFESLESSONS** from the book *Secrets,* discuss and then complete the following questions.

> *T*he teacher will always be silent especially when you are going through life's hardships and tests. You will have to remember the lessons you were taught and apply them!

1. Recall and describe one of the teachers who may have had a great impact on your life. Discuss.

_____
_____
_____
_____

b. Talk about an experience that you may have had where you felt alone and did not have the answers at first.

_____
_____
_____
_____
_____
_____
_____

2. Jesus is the Ultimate - The Greatest Teacher. Have you given Him your life and trusted Him as Lord and Savior? If not, repeat this simple prayer. Then, you must identify a Bible teaching church where you can grow and be taught the uncompromised Word of God.

Prayer For Salvation

Dear Lord, I know that I am a sinner. You died on the cross to set me free from the penalties of my sin. So right now, I ask You to come int my life and be Lord and Savior. Make me a brand new person. I denounce the devil. He will no longer have control over me because. You are now my Lord. Thank You for saving me. I love You Lord In Jesus name I pray, Amen.

"Beloved, do not think it strange, the fiery trial which is to try you, as though some strange thing happened to you..." – **1 Peter 4:12**

Secrets Every Mother Should Tell Her Daughter About Life! *Workbook*

Unlocking The SECRETS Code

Puzzles, Games, Activities

The Secrets Crossword Puzzle

Across

3. Wasting time or not making full use of the time given to you.

5. A noticeable change in nature, behavior, attitude, belief or character.

7. Hidden truths and principals which are not commonly known or obvious.

10. The act of being responsible for one's actions.

12. Strength and courage to endure to the end of a test, trial or difficult situation.

Down

1. The practice of being trained to follow certain rules and guideline.

2. An ability, chance or period of time given to you to accomplish something.

4. A predetermined course of events which are likely to happen.

6. The manner in which you think about, feel or approach something.

8. The achievement of a desired goal or result.

9. Personal objectives you desire to accomplish.

11. The abnormal use of something.

WORD LIST: Abuse, Attitude, Success, Procrastination, Accountability, Perseverance, Discipline, Destiny, Secrets, Transformation, Goals, Opportunity

And finally...whatsoever things are true,...honest,...just,...pure,...lovely,...of good report; if there be any virtue, and if there be any praise, think on these things.

Philippians 4:8

#YOURMIND#YOURTHOUGHTS#YOUR WORDS#YOURACTIONS

Congratulations!!!

You have successfully completed the

ecrets Every Mother Should Tell Her Daughter About Life! *Workbook*

Your signature below indicates that you are making a personal commitment, first to God and then yourself to live by the guidelines, morals and principles of the SECRETS pledge.

 **My SECRETS Pledge**

I, _____ (insert your name) do solemnly pledge to live my life according to the Word of God, and the principles and secrets uncovered in the SECRETS *book* and *workbook*. I willingly and freely make this pledge to fulfill God's divine purpose and plan for my life, accomplish my goals, and aggressively pursue my destiny while I live my best life ever!

This _____ day of _____, in the year _____ AD.

Signature: _____

Certificate of Participation

is awarded to

_____

on behalf of

The Faith Village For Girls Transformation Program

The "SECRETS" Tranformation Module

this _____ day of _____, _____ (A.D.)

Signed: _____

(Dr. Mattie Nottage, Youth Ambassador/Life Coach)

Pre-order your copy...

Secrets Every Mother Should Tell Her Daughter About Life! JOURNAL

****

Secrets Every Parent Should Tell Their Child About Life!

&

A Mother's Book Of Prayer For Her Children!

Coming Soon!

****

From Author of the best-selling book

Breaking The Chains, From Worship To Warfare

To request Dr. Mattie Nottage for a speaking engagement, upcoming event, life coaching seminar or mentorship session for girls or to place an order for products, please contact:

Mattie Nottage Ministries, International (Bahamas Address)
P.O. Box SB-52524
Nassau, N. P. Bahamas
Tel/Fax (242) 698-1383
Or **(954) 237-8196**

OR

Mattie Nottage Ministries, International (U.S. Address)
6511 Nova Dr., Suite #193
Davie, Florida 33317

Tel/Fax: **(888) 825-7568**
UK Tel: 44 (0) 203371 9922

OR

www.mattienottage.org

Journal Notes

www.ingramcontent.com/pod-product-compliance
Lightning Source LLC
Chambersburg PA
CBHW040906020526
44114CB00037B/75